DATE DUE			

2748

599.74
HO

Hoffman, Mary.

Wild dog.

DISCARD

PLEASANT GLADE ELEM. SCHOOL

Animals in the Wild

Wild Dog

by Mary Hoffman

Raintree Childrens Books
Milwaukee
Belitha Press Limited • London

Have you ever seen a litter of puppies? These are fox pups, only five days old. Like dog puppies, they are blind and deaf. Foxes and wolves are wild relatives of the common dog.

These are coyote pups. Coyote pups, like other pups in the dog family, can see quite well after about two weeks. But they still stay hidden in their den for some time.

Dogs are good mothers. The mother feeds her babies with her milk while they are small. Many babies are born in one litter. Can you count how many pups this African hunting dog has?

Until a puppy can move as fast as its mother,
the quickest way for it to travel is in her mouth!
This African hunting dog is taking her pup
from one den to another, perhaps a safer one.

Once they are old enough to leave the den,
wild dogs like to explore. These little jackals
from Africa are coming out for a good look
around.

Often, wild dogs live together in groups, called packs. When these jackal pups grow older, they may stay with their parents to help look after the next litter.

Dogs are not always friendly with one another.
These two African hunting dogs are fighting for
the same piece of meat. They have killed a
gazelle and are fighting over their share.

But usually a pack of dogs shares its food. All dogs are carnivores, which means they are meat-eaters. Dogs that hunt in packs can kill animals much bigger than themselves.

Most wolves live in packs. They may be quite small—only seven or eight animals. Wolves let other wolves know where they are by howling. They also seem to enjoy it as a social activity!

All members of the dog family have a good
sense of smell. This wolf is checking the tree
for another wolf's scent. Each wolf has its own
place in the pack. There is always a leader.

13

Foxes don't live in packs. Fox pups stay with their parents until they can hunt for themselves. This male and female fox are fighting just outside a den.

There are more than twenty different kinds of foxes. The red fox is the largest. It lives in America, Europe, Asia, and Africa. It is hunted by people because it kills small farm animals.

15

This arctic fox lives near the North Pole. In summer, its fur is a brownish-gray color. But it turns white in the winter and blends in with the snow.

Foxes also live as far south as southern Africa.
Here their coats are colored like their sandy
background. Cape foxes are much smaller
than their red or arctic relations.

The bat-eared fox lives in Africa. Its big ears help it to keep cool because it loses body heat through them. The bat-eared fox feeds mostly on insects.

The fennec fox lives in the desert in Africa and has the biggest ears of all! But it is the smallest member of the dog family. It weighs only two to three pounds.

Coyotes weigh about ten times as much as
fennec foxes. But wolves are even larger—males
may weigh 100 pounds or more. Wolves hunt in
packs, but most coyotes live alone or in pairs.

Coyotes look like ordinary dogs and so does the dingo, the wild dog of Australia. Both can mate with tame dogs. Dingoes live in packs and sometimes hunt together.

The maned wolf is called a wolf because of its large size, but it looks more like a red fox with long legs. It lives in South America. Its long legs help it move easily in the tall grass.

The tame dog is called "man's best friend," but people are usually the wild dog's enemy. Foxes are hunted and killed for sport. But some foxes live in towns and feed on garbage.

First published in this edition in the United States of America 1987
by Raintree Publishers Inc., 310 West Wisconsin Avenue,
Milwaukee, Wisconsin 53203.

First published in the United Kingdom under the title
Animals in the Wild—Wild Dog
by Belitha Press Ltd.,
31 Newington Green, London N16 9PU
in association with Methuen Children's Books Ltd.

Library of Congress Number: 86-17779

Dedicated to Liam, Sam and Carly.

Scientific Adviser: Dr. Gwynne Vevers. Picture Researcher: Stella Martin.
Design: Ken Hatherley.

Acknowledgements are due to the following for the photographs used
in this book: Bruce Coleman Ltd pp. 1, 3, 6, 8, 10-11, 12, 16, 18, 21, 22
and 23; Oxford Scientific Films Ltd pp. 9, 15, 20 and front cover; Frank
Lane Picture Agency pp. 2, 7, 13, 14 and back cover; Survival Anglia p. 4;
NHPA p. 17; David Hosking p. 19.

ISBN 0-8172-2704-0

Library of Congress Cataloging in Publication Data

Hoffman, Mary, 1945-
  Wild dog.

  (Animals in the wild)
  Summary: Text and photographs describe the behavior
and habitats of wild dogs.
    1. Canidae—Juvenile literature.   2. Wild dogs—
Juvenile literature.   [1. Canidae.   2. Wild dogs]
I. Title.   II. Series.
QL737.C22H62   1987   599.74'422   86-17779
ISBN 0-8172-2704-0

1 2 3 4 5 6 7 8 9   90 89 88 87 86